Date: _______________

*Created especially for you*

Date: ______________________________

Created especially for you

Everyone needs
'A Little Black Book'.
A place to write 'secret
things' and to write 'stuff'
that you think about and
want to remember - and
not want to remember.
'A Little Black Book' is that
prized and treasured
notebook
that you keep close to your
heart.
The 'Little Black Book' that
takes you on journeys of
memories - and prepares
you for the next one.
Everything you need will be
in here.

# Created especially for
# you.....

Date: _______________________

Date: _______________________

Created especially for you

Date: _______________________

Date: ______________________________

*Created especially for you*

# Date: _______________________

*Created especially for you*

Date: ____________________________

Created especially for you

Date: _______________

Date: _______________________________

# Date:

Date: ______________________________________________

Date: _______________________________

Date: _______________________

Date: ____________________

Date: _______________

Date: _______________________

*Created especially for you*

Date: _______________________

Date: ___________________________

Date: ___________________________

Created especially for you

Date: ___________________

Date: ______________________

Created especially for you

Date: ________________________________

Date: _______________

Date: _______________________

_Created especially for you_

Date:

Date: _______________________________

*Created especially for you*

Date:

Created especially for you

Date: ______________________________

Created especially for you

Date: _______________________________

Created especially for you

Date: ____________________________

Date: ______________________

Created especially for you

Date: ___________________________

Date: _______________________

Date: ___________________

Date: _______________________

Date: _______________________

# Date: _______________

## Date: _______________________

_Created especially for you_

Date: _______________________

*Created especially for you*

Date: _______________________________

Created especially for you

# Date: ___________________

Date: ____________________

Date: _______________________________

Date: ___________________________

Created especially for you

Date: ________________________________

Date: _______________________

Created especially for you

Date: ___________________________

Date: _______________________________

Created especially for you

Date: _______________________

*Created especially for you*

Date: ____________________________

Created especially for you

Date: _______________

Date: _______________

Date: _______________________________

Date: ________________________

*Created especially for you*

Date: _______________________

Created especially for you

Date: ___________________________________________

Date: _______________________

Date: _______________

Date: ___________________

*Created especially for you*

Date: ______________________

Date: _______________________

Date: _______________________

Date: _______________________

Date: ______________________________

Created especially for you

Date:

Created especially for you

Date: _______________________

*Created especially for you*

# Date: ______________________________

*Created especially for you*

Date: _______________________________

Date: _______________________________

Created especially for you

Date: _______________________________

# Date: _______________

Date: ______________________________________

Created especially for you

# Date: _______________

Date: ___________________________________________

Created especially for you

Date: ___________________________________

*Created especially for you*

Date: _______________

Date: _______________________

Date: _______________________________

Date: _______________________

Created especially for you

Date: _______________________

Date:

Created especially for you

Date: _______________________________

Created especially for you

# Date: ___________________________

Date: _______________

Date:

Created especially for you

Date: _______________________________

_Created especially for you_

Date: _______________

*Created especially for you*

Date:

Date: ______________________________

Created especially for you

Date: _______________

Date: _______________________________

Date: _______________________________

Created especially for you

Date: _______________________________

Date: _______________

Created especially for you

Date: _______________________

Date: _______________________

Date:

Date: _______________________

Created especially for you

Date: ______________________________

_Created especially for you_

Date: _______________________________

*Created especially for you*

Date: _______________________

Date: _______________

Date: ______________________

Date: _______________________________

Created especially for you

Date: _______________________________

*Created especially for you*

Date: _______________________________

*Created especially for you*

Date: _______________________________

*Created especially for you*

Date: _______________________________

*Created especially for you*

Date: ___________________________________________

Date: ______________________________

*Created especially for you*

Date: _______________

Date: _______________________________

Created especially for you

Date: _______________

Created especially for you

Date: _______________________

Date: ______________________________

Date: _______________

Date: _______________________

Date: _______________________

Date: _______________________

Date: _______________________________

Date: ____________________

Date: ______________________________

Created especially for you

# Date: _______________

_Created especially for you_

Date: _______________________

*Created especially for you*

Date:

Date: ___________________________

Date: _______________________________

Created especially for you

Date: ______________________________________________________

_Created especially for you_

Date: _______________

_Created especially for you_

# Date: ___________

Date: ____________________

Date: ______________________

Created especially for you

Date: _______________________________

Created especially for you

Date: ______________________________

Date: _______________________

Date: ___________________________________

Date: _______________________________

Created especially for you

Date: ______________________

Date: _______________________________

Created especially for you

Date: _______________________

Date: _______________________

Date: _______________________

Date: ______________________________

Date:

Date: _______________________

Date: ________________________________

Created especially for you

Date: _______________________________

Created especially for you

Date: ________________

Created especially for you

Date: _______________________

Created especially for you

Date: ______________________________

Date: _______________________________

Created especially for you

Date: ___________________

Date: ___________________

Date: _______________________

Created especially for you

Date: ________________________________

# Date: _______________

Date: ______________________________________

Created especially for you

Date: _______________________________

Date: ______________________________

Created especially for you

Date: _______________________

*Created especially for you*

Date: ______________________________

Date: _______________________________

Date: ___________________

Date: _______________________________

Date: _______________________________

*Created especially for you*

Date: _______________________________

Created especially for you

# Date: _______________

Date: ____________________

Date: _______________________

Date: _______________________

Date: _______________________________

Date: _______________________

Date:

Created especially for you

Date: _______________________

Created especially for you

Date: _______________________________

*Created especially for you*

Date: _______________________________